ENGINEERING CHALLENGES

BUILDING RACE CARS

by Samantha S. Bell

FOCUS READERS

WWW.FOCUSREADERS.COM

Focus Readers is distributed by North Star Editions:
sales@northstareditions.com | 888-417-0195

Produced for Focus Readers by Red Line Editorial.

Content Consultant: David Bennett, retired engineer and entrepreneur

Photographs ©: tcharts/Shutterstock Images, cover, 1; Action Sports Photography/Shutterstock Images, 4–5, 15, 16; Bain News Service/Bain Collection/Library of Congress, 7; HodagMedia/Shutterstock Images, 9, 10–11; Natursports/Shutterstock Images, 13; Walter G. Arce Sr./Cal Sport Media/AP Images, 18–19; John Raoux/AP Images, 21; Marco Vasini/AP Images, 23; Red Line Editorial, 24–25, 26, 29

ISBN
978-1-63517-254-6 (hardcover)
978-1-63517-319-2 (paperback)
978-1-63517-449-6 (ebook pdf)
978-1-63517-384-0 (hosted ebook)

Library of Congress Control Number: 2017935923

Printed in the United States of America
Mankato, MN
June, 2017

ABOUT THE AUTHOR

Samantha S. Bell is the author of more than 50 nonfiction books for children. She lives with her family and lots of pets in South Carolina near NASCAR's Greenville-Pickens Speedway.

TABLE OF CONTENTS

CHAPTER 1

RACING FROM THE START

The first gasoline-powered automobile was built around 1885. Ten years later, in 1895, Émile Levassor became the first car racing champion. The course was more than 700 miles (1,127 km) across France. Levassor averaged only 15 miles per hour (24 km/h). And he finished in just under 49 hours.

The first race cars were no match for those of today.

Much has changed since that 1895 race. But cars and racing are still very much connected. Race cars are automobiles specifically designed for speed. Drivers compete in races around the world to see who is the fastest. Today's cars can go faster than 200 miles per hour (322 km/h). Yet all are designed to keep the drivers as safe as possible.

The car industry was still new in the early 1900s. Racing proved to be a good way for companies to show off their new cars. Henry Ford used a race car in 1902 to show off his design skills. He went on to start what is now Ford Motor Company. Race cars have long had the

Fans check out a race car before a 1918 race in New York.

best available technology. Many new
features were first demonstrated at
racetracks. Indianapolis Motor Speedway
is a famous track. It opened in 1909.

In the 1920s, people began racing
their personal cars. These are called
stock cars. But auto racing came to a halt
during World War II (1939–1945). Cars
were only produced for the war effort.

Racing began again after the war ended. Race organizers created the National Association for Stock Car Auto Racing (NASCAR). This group organized stock car racing on oval tracks throughout the southern United States.

After World War II, the fastest European race cars became known as Formula One cars. On these cars, the wheels are exposed with no **fenders**. This is called open wheel. Their races were mostly on closed-off roads. The fastest open-wheel cars in the United States were called IndyCars. They were known for racing the Indianapolis 500. It began in 1911 at Indianapolis Motor Speedway.

Open-wheel IndyCars compete at a race in Iowa.

Today, Formula One cars race all over the world. These cars race on special racetracks. NASCAR races are held at tracks in North America. IndyCars race on many of these same tracks. However, stock cars and IndyCars never compete in the same races.

CHAPTER 2

FAST AND FASTER

Engineers design different types of cars depending on the racing style. Stock cars look like the cars we see on the road. However, stock cars have added features for both speed and protection. Formula One and IndyCars are single-seat cars. Their wheels are outside of the main body. Their engines are in the rear.

IndyCars are designed specifically for racing.

Racing leagues set basic guidelines for the cars. Each car must meet a minimum weight, maximum engine size, maximum width, and minimum height. Engineers and designers aim to make the fastest cars they can within those rules.

Some design principles apply to all cars. As a car moves, high-pressure air pushes on it from the front. The car must push the air out of the way. Meanwhile, the path the air takes as it goes over the car can create lift. This is a force that can pull the car off the ground. Therefore, engineers create **aerodynamic** designs in an effort to reduce the **drag** and increase the **downforce**.

Formula One cars stay close to the ground.

Added downforce increases the ground pressure and therefore the grip. Grip is also called traction. Increased traction improves both **acceleration** and cornering speed. Traction comes from the force the tire applies against the ground. Most racing tires are completely smooth. Each tire's entire surface can touch the track, giving the tires better grip.

Formula One and IndyCars are faster than stock cars. These cars have a smaller frontal area. It is the part of the car that pushes through the air. This makes the cars more aerodynamic. A rear engine allows the driver to sit lower in the car. Because of the lower **center of gravity**, the driver can go faster around corners without the car's wheels lifting. This keeps the car from rolling over.

Rear-engine cars also have better traction. Having more engine weight in the rear increases the ground pressure on the back wheels. This means more power can be used for acceleration and cornering before the back tires lose grip.

Stock cars race at NASCAR's Daytona 500.

Engineers have options for improving their cars. For example, they can increase acceleration by reducing weight, increasing power, or both. In addition, some rules allow for special parts or designs to be added to cars. Some cars can have upside-down wings at the front or back. These wings create downforce.

NASCAR requires special safety equipment in each car.

Designers can also shape the car to create a **vacuum** effect under the car. This also increases downforce. The spoiler attached to the front of stock cars can also cause this vacuum.

Engineers also add safety features to protect drivers. These can include harnesses, **fuel cells**, removable seats, padding, and head and neck restraints.

ENGINEERING DESIGN PROCESS

Engineers use many tools and computer programs in their planning. Once a race car is built, engineers perform many tests in the shop and on the track to prove that the design meets their expectations.

ASK: What type of race will the car compete in? How can the car's acceleration and cornering speed be improved? How can the car be made more aerodynamic? What can be added to protect the driver?

IMAGINE: Brainstorm possible car designs. What design would give the car the fastest acceleration?

PLAN: Draw a diagram of the car. Make a list of materials needed. Write down a list of steps.

CREATE: Follow the plan and build a race car.

IMPROVE: What worked with the car? What did not work? Change your design to make the car faster.

CHAPTER 3

THE FORD GT

In 2016, Ford entered its new GT in the Rolex 24 race in Daytona, Florida. The car had many advanced features. The aerodynamic design produced more downforce for faster cornering, better stability, and less drag. The car had a strong, light **chassis** and a powerful new V6 engine.

The No. 66 Ford GT races in the 2016 Rolex 24.

The Rolex 24 is a 24-hour race. Ford entered the No. 66 and No. 67 cars. But just 16 minutes in, No. 67 began having trouble. The car lost speed and would not shift correctly. It had to be taken to the garage to be fixed. Then the car had more problems. A diffuser, used to help create vacuum downforce, was damaged. It rubbed against one of the car's tires, cutting it two times. Crews had to replace part of the car's transmission. No. 66 had transmission problems, too. Soon both cars were too far behind to catch up.

Ford had expected to win the race with one of the cars. Neither ended in the top five of its class. But the team learned a

The No. 67 Ford GT races in 2017.

lot about the new GT. And they knew what they needed to fix for next time.

Ford entered the cars into the 2017 Rolex 24 race. No. 66 often took the lead during the first few hours. Cold and wet weather conditions made the nighttime driving difficult, but No. 66 pushed to the front again and again. The GT finished first in its category and fifth overall.

THE FERRARI SF70H

Formula One cars must follow certain rules in their designs. In 2017, some major changes were made in the rules. The car bodies and tires had to be wider. This improved downforce and traction. The rear wings also had to be wider and lower.

Ferrari did not win a single race in 2016. So in 2017, engineers used the new rules to build a better car. They created the Ferrari SF70H. It had a sharply-angled front and a longer nose. This made it more aerodynamic. Designers also added a shark fin to the engine cover. It helped move air away from the new rear wing, especially while the car was going around corners.

The car did well in practice, but the true test was on the track. The new design was a success!

Sebastian Vettel drives the new Ferrari SF70H in 2017.

In the opening race of the 2017 season, the Ferrari SF70H won by nearly 10 seconds.

CHAPTER 4

BUILD A RACE CAR!

Engineers build superfast race cars with top-of-the-line equipment. Use household products to make your own!

Materials:

Use a toilet paper tube, two straws, and four spools with or without thread to make your car. Masking tape, a pen, and a ruler can help put everything together.

You can build your own simple car with a few common objects.

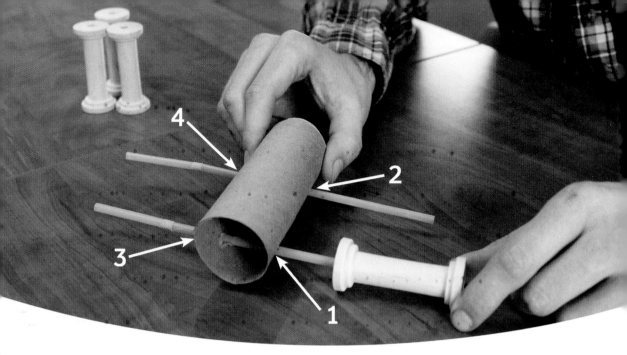

The straws can work as axles for your car.

Procedure:

1. With a ruler, draw a straight line from one opening of the toilet paper tube to the other. Measure 1 inch (2.5 cm) from one end. Mark this spot on your line as "#1." Then measure 1 inch from the other side. Mark this spot on the line as "#2."

2. Turn the toilet paper tube so the openings are to the side. Place the end of the ruler at #1. Roll the tube. Make a mark 2 inches (5 cm) away. Label this mark "#3." Then do the same from #2. Label this one "#4."

3. Use the tip of your pen to punch holes in the toilet paper tube at each of the four marks.

4. Push a straw through mark #1 and mark #3. The straw should stick out from the sides of the toilet paper tube. Push another straw through mark #2 and mark #4. These are your axles. An axle is the bar that a wheel revolves around.

5. Remove any labels from the spools of thread. Slide one spool onto each of the four straws. To secure the spools, add a small piece of masking tape to the end of each straw.

6. Test your race car! Try rolling it on a smooth surface, such as a table.

Improve It!

- The car is shaped like a cylinder. How can you change its shape to make it more aerodynamic?

- Use the tape to make a starting line and a finish line. Push the car to make it roll. With a friend's help, use a stopwatch to see how fast the car goes. How can you make it faster?

This car uses a longer paper towel tube and has an aerodynamic front.

- Try using different materials for the body of the race car, such as paper cups or a plastic water bottle. Which materials work the best?

FOCUS ON
BUILDING RACE CARS

Write your answers on a separate piece of paper.

1. Write a letter to a friend describing the main ideas of Chapter 2.

2. Formula One cars look a lot different from stock cars. Which type of race car do you like best? Why?

3. What is one way engineers can improve acceleration?

    A. by reducing the power to the driving wheels
    B. by reducing the traction of the tires
    C. by reducing the car's weight

4. What do engineers try to limit when designing race cars?

    A. downforce
    B. lift
    C. traction

Answer key on page 32.

GLOSSARY

acceleration
The process of moving faster.

aerodynamic
The qualities of an object that affect how easily it is able to move through the air.

center of gravity
The average center of all of an object's weight.

chassis
The frame of a motor vehicle.

downforce
A force produced by air resistance that pushes down on a vehicle.

drag
A force that opposes motion, usually air resistance or rolling friction.

fenders
Guards that cover a car's wheels.

fuel cells
Rubber sacs inside a fuel tank that limit leakage if the fuel tank is punctured.

vacuum
A space without air.

TO LEARN MORE

BOOKS

Gregory, Josh. *Race Cars: Science, Technology, Engineering*. New York: Children's Press, 2015.

Kenney, Karen Latchana. *The Science of Car Racing*. North Mankato, MN: Capstone Press, 2014.

Silverman, Buffy. *How Do Formula One Race Cars Work?* Minneapolis: Lerner Publications, 2016.

NOTE TO EDUCATORS

Visit **www.focusreaders.com** to find lesson plans, activities, links, and other resources related to this title.

INDEX

Answer Key: 1. Answers will vary; **2.** Answers will vary; **3.** C; **4.** B